D1134428

To my mum
with much love
Christine
x x x x x

For a Special Mum

on Mothers Day
2003

For a
Special Mum

A *Heartwarmers*™
Gift Book

For a Special Mum
A Heartwarmers™ Gift Book

©WPL 2002

Text by Andrea Coleman, Beth Waters, Shirley Collins,
Julie Ellis, Stephanie Baudet, Carrie Hewlett,
Barbara Manning, E. Floyd and Pauline Jones
Illustration by Jo Parry - Advocate

Printed in China
Published by WPL 2002

ISBN 1-904264-12-3

For information on other Heartwarmers™ gift books,
gifts and greetings cards, please contact
WPL
14 Victoria Ind. Est. Wales Farm Road
London W3 6UU UK
Tel: +44 (0) 208 993 7268 Fax: +44 (0) 208 993 8041
email: wpl@atlas.co.uk

Mums are the most
important people in our lives.
Their support, love and care help us
through the ups and downs of life, and their
kindness and devotion inspire us all.
This unique collection of poems is a
tribute to Mums everywhere.

Mum

your cheerful smile
and thoughtful, caring ways,
bring happiness to my life
and sunshine to my days.

Pauline Jones

Thanks Mum

There's so much to thank you for
from the moment of my birth.
You've cherished, loved and cared for me
more than anyone on earth.

Thanks for every thoughtful gift,
each lovingly chosen treat -
for the simple, yet important things
like clothes and food to eat.

You've nursed me through life's problems
with unflagging love and care,
and it never failed to comfort me
knowing you were there.

Thanks for everything you've given,
each sacrifice you make,
your boundless love and selflessness,
and the extra steps you take.

I know I haven't always shown
how much I appreciate your care,
but I want you to know I love you, Mum,
for always being there.

Andrea Coleman

Thanks for being you

Mum you taught me so very much
and waited patiently,
as I learnt and as I grew
you watched over me.

You showed me so many things,
opened wide a magic door,
to a big wide world of wonders
to search and to explore.

You listened to my problems
and always helped me through,
so thank you Mum for everything
and thanks for being You !

Barbara Manning

The world's best Mum

I am really lucky
to have a Mum like you,
and though I don't
often tell you
I'm so grateful
for all that you do.

Intuitively you have always known
how to help and what to say,
and you've always been there for me
at any time of day.

Thanks for all your thoughtfulness
your humour in all that you do.
Whatever life throws at you
your sunny nature shines through.

And so, Mum, I just want to say
you're not just my special chum,
best of all you see is that
you are the world's best Mum.

Carrie Hewlett

I've learned so much from you

I know I don't always tell you, Mum,
but there's something I just want to say,
without your love I'd never have become
the person I am today.

You're more than just a Mum to me,
you're my teacher, my guide and my friend.
You're everything you could possibly be
which is why I want to send...

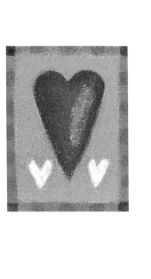

...grateful thanks for all you've done,
your guidance, your patience and care,
but most of all, above all else,
Mum, thanks for being there.

Julie Ellis

Me & My Mum

As wide as the ocean
as deep as the sea,
as high as the heavens
is your love for me.

As deep as the sunset
as high as the sky,
as high as the mountains
you taught me to fly.

As quiet as a whisper
as loud as a drum,
together forever
just me and my Mum.

E. Floyd

You're my inspiration

Ever since I can remember, Mum,
I've longed to be like you.
You've always inspired me
in everything I do.

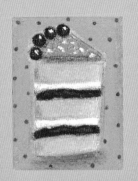

More than anyone I know
I've looked up to and admired you,
for you have every quality
that I have long aspired to.

Your great sense of humour,
your intelligence and wit,
are matched by warmth and kindness
courage, strength and grit.

It's not just through your merits
that you have inspired and guided me,
you've nurtured me and helped me find
the qualities inside me.

You've shown me what love and honesty
and friendship are about.
You've instilled in me real self-belief
and taught me not to doubt.

With your example I can cope
with any situation,
you've taught me
how to live and love,
Mum, you're my inspiration.

Andrea Coleman

You're a star

Mum you are a shining star
though the world doesn't know your name.
You have no fancy title
like Baroness or Dame.

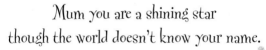

You've never won an Oscar
or a literary prize,
but, dear Mum, you'll always be
a winner in my eyes.

Mum you really are a star
my mother, mentor and friend.
A Nobel prize for motherhood
is what I'd recommend.

You may not be famous,
as your face is known to few,
but Mum I think you're wonderful
and I'm so proud of you.

Stephanie Baudet

You're my best mate

If I could give you everything
as thanks for being my Mum,
I'd give you all of life's nice things -
rainbows, blue skies and sun.

And if I won the lottery
I'd share my win with you.
I'd take you on a spending spree
each day the whole year through.

You're the best Mum anyone's had
the Mum I'd pick myself.
You outshine other Mums and Dads
and everybody else.

So thank you, Mum, for being you,
for simply being great,
for good advice when I am blue
and for being my best mate.

Beth Waters

You're a great Mum

It's wonderful to have a Mum
as good at it as you.
You make it look so easy
in all the things you do.

You're always there to talk to,
a great source of advice.
You're very good at listening
which makes confiding nice.

You're always kind and helpful
and I rarely hear you moan.
You are the firm foundation
upon which I have grown.

You're the best example
of how a Mum should be,
and every day in every way
you mean so much to me.

Beth Waters

Mums are precious

Some things in life are priceless,
they cannot be bought or sold.
The uniqueness of a mother's love
is a gift more precious than gold.

Your humour and your tenderness
are things I'll always treasure.
My love for you is endless,
and your worth is beyond all measure.

Julie Ellis

You're my special friend

I'm grateful you are there for me
with your love and support,
but I've never really thanked you
quite as often as I ought.

I want to thank you, Mum,
from the bottom of my heart.
Because of you my life got off
to the very best of starts.

As each year goes rolling by
with more happy memories made,
my love for you grows deeper
in new and different ways.

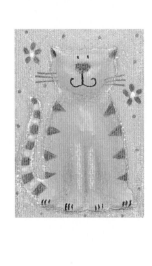

It is something very special
the bond that we both share,
but I rarely get the chance
to tell you how much I care.

I love you with all my heart, Mum,
and today I want to send,
my thanks for all you've done for me
and for being my special friend.

Shirley Collins